MEMORIES

MEMORIES

Mary Elizabeth Chapman

Prospect Press
Sistersville
West Virginia

Published by Prospect Press
609 Main Street
Sistersville, West Virginia 26175

Library of Congress Catalog Card Number:
    98-068387

ISBN: 1-892668-08-4

Manufactured in the United States of America

First Edition

10 9 8 7 6 5 4 3 2 1

DEDICATION

To My Parents:
Thomas J. Johnson
(June 8, 1881—July 15, 1973)
            and
Amelia Maulsby Johnson
(December 9, 1883—September 12, 1970)

To My Sister, Marjorie Marie Johnson
(January 1, 1916—January 25, 1962)

To My Husband, Lawrence K. Chapman
(December 15, 1899—July 22, 1974)

CONTENTS

Section I

Section II

MEMORIES

Section I

Standing at the end of the old country lane
Just at the close of the day
That's when memories of days long gone by
Hold full sway.

The big red barn is silent and still
But I know all is well
And off in the distance I faintly hear
The tinkle of the old cow bell.

The chickens so busy in the barnyard at noon
Under the shining sun
Have quietly slipped off to roost
One by one.

The hogs in the lot
Squealed and grunted 'til fed
Have settled for a night of repose
In a soft mud bed.

Rays from the moon
Creep slowly down the hill
To bathe in silver
The world so peaceful and still.

The stars come out
One by one
To twinkle in the sky
Until the night is done.

REMEMBERING

Sad and lonely
And feeling blue
Sitting all alone
Thinking of you.

Miss your smile
And tender embrace
No other one
Can take your place.

Our time together
Was just twelve years
Some days were sunny
While others held tears.

It's been twenty-four years
Since you went away
And I miss you more and more
With each passing day.

August 1, 1998

To the town of Bethlehem
Many years ago
Joseph came with Mary
Riding a donkey gentle and slow.

Mary was tired
The journey had been long
She wanted a place to rest
Away from the pressing throng.

But little Bethlehem
Was crowded that night you see
With people paying the tax
Ordered by Caesar's decree

Joseph tried again and again
By knocking on every door
Only to hear the same refrain
We have no room for more.

'Til at last an innkeeper
Called after the departing pair
I have a stable in the back
You're welcome to stay in there.

So to the rude stable
Mary and Joseph went
The day was done
And the night was far spent.

There during the night
Without a sound
The Baby Jesus was born
With friendly animals all around.

Out on the hillside
That very same night
Shepherds watching their flocks
Were startled by a Heavenly light.

While they knelt on the hillside
Bowed down with fear
A Heavenly Angel
To them did appear.

Do not be afraid
The Angel said
You'll find the Saviour
Sleeping in a manger bed.

They left their sheep
And away they sped
To see if it were true
As the Angel had said.

In another country
Away off afar
Certain Wise Men were
Watching a bright new star.

The star they followed
Up hill and down
Until they finally arrived
At Bethlehem Town.

Shepherds and Wise Men
And animals too
Gathered around the manger
The Baby to view.

Then let's do now
As they did then
Offer a prayer
For Peace on Earth, Good Will to Men.

The Festival of Booth
Is here again
Giving a chance to aid and cheer
Our fellowman.

Early in the fall
Items collected by the youth
Are put on display
In an attractive booth.

Food and clothing
And school supplies too
Are neatly arranged
For all to view.

Prizes are given
One, two, three
For the best idea
Worked out for all to see.

At the close of the Festival
With its work and fun
We know the joy
Of a job well done.

The Lambert's Run youth
Were glad to do our part
Our work and what we gave
Came from the heart.

The Bible in Genesis Chapter One
Tells us how the world was begun

In the beginning all was dark
God said, "Let there be light,"
And it was so
The light became day
The darkness night
On that first day.

There were waters everywhere
God made the firmament
To separate waters above
From those below
The firmament became Heaven
On the second day.

The waters together became seas
The dry land became Earth
With grass, herbs and fruit trees
Yielding seed after its own kind
On the third day.

Two great lights in the firmament of Heaven
Separated day from night
The greater ruled day
The lesser ruled night
On the fourth day.

Creatures were made to live in the water
The fowl to fly above earth
Each one was blessed
To be fruitful and multiply
On the fifth day.

God made man in his own image
He created Male and Female
To multiply and replenish the earth
And have dominion over fish in the sea
Fowl of the air and every living
Thing that moveth upon the earth
His work was completed the sixth day

After the heavens and earth were finished
God rested the seventh day
That was the day He blessed and sanctified
Because it was His rest day.

In the beginning all was darkness
Then God made the light
A sun for the day
A moon for the night.

God made the firmament
Where waters did abound
To separate the seas
From the dry ground.

Be fruitful and multiply
Was God's command
To creatures in the sea
And those on dry land.

Two great lights in Heaven
Furnished the light
The sun for the day
The moon for the night.

The creatures in the water
And fowl above earth
Were all blessed by God
Who established their worth.

In His own image
God created man
And we're all a part
Of His great plan.

Then let's all do
The best that we can
To live in harmony
With our fellowman.

It is with an air of sadness
That we look back at the past
Where we spent such happy times together
And made some friendships that will last.

Now comes the time for our departure
And we know not what lies ahead
But always we'll endeavor
To do our best wherever we are led.

October 1982

How it grieves my heart today
As I travel the King's Highway
To see one person mistreat another
Treat him less than as a brother.

God gave different talents
A fact that is true
Let me try things my way
I'll do likewise by you.

Nothing can hurt another more
Or make a failure complete
Than to grumble in the back of the room
Or sit in the scorner's seat.

Then without grumble or complaint
Let me try my wings
The same courtesy I'll return to you
When you step out to do your things.

Did you ever stop to think
The unkind acts you do
May hurt someone today
And return twofold to you?

Little acts of spite
That cause another pain
May make the feeling between brothers
Never quite the same again.

So keep a bridle on your thoughts
A check upon your tongue
So you won't regret when old
The acts you did when young.

Did you ever stop to think
As you sit there in your chair
That your face reveals your inner thoughts
Of happiness or despair?

If your face is bright and sunny
And your eyes are shining too
It shows that you are happy
As life's pathway you pursue.

If your face is gray and sullen
And your eyes lack luster too
That's a very good indication
Unhappiness has its grip on you.

If on your face you wear a frown
And your eyes are piercing and sharp
Folks won't gather around you
'Cause on anything they mention you'll harp.

If you would be happy
And make others happy too
Keep a song in your heart
Smile, God loves you.

Our Father in Heaven
Who looks down from above
Admonishes us all
To show brotherly love.

He gave us a rule
That is golden it's true
You treat me as
You want me to treat you.

He gave us talents
Some large and some small
That He expects to be used
By one and all.

If a brother with a talent small
Is doing his best
You can be sure
That by our Father he'll be blest.

I love the early morning
When the grass with dew is pearled
In this calm and peaceful stillness
All is right within my world.

If I stand a moment longer
Just taking in the view
Then my strength will be replenished
For the tasks which I must do.

For each day's a new beginning
And we know not what 'twill bring
If our eyes will fill with teardrops
Or in our hearts we'll sing.

Then let us take a moment longer
To be sure that things go right
Say a prayer that God will guide us
Through the day and through the night.

May 14, 1984

November 10th, 1982
A day long remembered
By me and you
When 51 participants
Came our new site to view
And enjoyed a delicious meal
Prepared by our faithful crew
As we look back
Just one year after
We remember the friendships
Joy and laughter
And now we look forward
With joy in our heart
To a brand new year
About to start.

AN ENDING AND NEW BEGINNING

Participants leaving the nutrition site
Tuesday, June 28, 1994
Remembered in review
Our arrival November 10, 1982

As we look back
Just twelve years after
We remember the friendships
Joy and laughter.

Some with us at that time
Are still with us today
While others for one reason or another
Have had to go away.

With thanks for donations
And volunteer skill
Our new site will open
On High School Hill
Tuesday, July 5, 1994

Early in the morning
Just before the clock strikes five
The quiet, reverent stillness
Makes me glad to be alive

Far off in the distance
A bird begins to trill
As the light of early morning
Creeps slowly down the hill.

Soon a ray of golden sunlight
Laughing dewdrops on the grass
Creates a field of sparkling diamonds
To be seen by those who chance to pass.

The babble of the brook
Flowing down its pebble bed
Reflects golden sunlight on the water
And a sky of blue o'er head.

Their still and quiet beauty
That's a part of Nature's plan
Can strengthen our resolve
To live peacefully with our fellowman.

When the day is dark and cloudy
And the sky is overcast
Then I like to sit and ponder
On bright things of the past.

Of the bright sun on the water
That reflects the sky of blue
Then it is in memory
My thoughts return to you.

How we walked the path together
Among flowers of every hue
And I remember every moment
Of the hours I spent with you.

Gone but not forgotten
Are the times we used to share
And the happy memories linger
'Tis for them I'll always care.

August 25, 1982

The fairies did their wash last night
And hung it out to dry
I saw the tiny bits of lace
This morning as I passed by.

Some pieces were hung upon the fence
A beauty to behold
And when the sun began to shine
Reflected hues of gold.

Some they spread upon the grass
For all who pass by to view
The tiny masterpiece of diamonds
Etched in by the dew.

And when this lovely sight I see
In the early morning light
I am thoroughly convinced
They must have worked all night.

August 7, 1980

When autumn leaves begin to fall
Then it is that I recall
The sunny days of summer
That we knew.

Strolling down the lane together
In both fair and stormy weather
Walking hand in hand
Just me and you.

Walking under skies of blue
Among flowers of every hue
As we did in days
When love was new.

Though those days are past and gone
Still the memories linger on
In the heart of one
Alone and blue.

Then from out of memory's store
I can live them o'er and o'er
Until I live them all again
With you.

October 1982

In the stillness of the morning
Just before the break of dawn
Is the time for recollection
And the planning to go on.

Though the road ahead is rocky
And the path sometimes grows dim
Everything can be much brighter
If you put your trust in Him.

If you see a troubled brother
As you travel through the land
You can lighten up his burden
With a kind and helping hand.

Perhaps a worried sister
Too weary to go another mile
May find her spirits lifted
By the sunshine of your smile.

We are on this earth together
By the Father's divine plan
So we must help each other
And do the best we can.

July 1994

I am sitting by the fireplace
Dreaming dreams of long ago
And the faces of my loved ones
I see in the embers' golden glow.

One by one the scenes pass by me
In which each one had a part
And these joys I'll always treasure
In the chambers of my heart.

When the day's been long and dreary
And my heart is filled with woe
Then in memory I can travel
To the happy scenes of long ago.

When my troubles begin to pile up
And that can't go on feeling I know
Then it's time for me to journey
To the happy times of long ago.

Then my world's a little calmer
And life takes on an added glow
When I return from memory's travel
To the happy scenes I used to know.

EXPECTATION

I like to think you're waiting
Near an open gate for me
And that again we'll be together
Just the way we used to be.

Where all our gray skies
Have turned a brilliant blue
And flowers along the roadside
Are blooming in every hue.

Where the days are warm and sunny
And we can really say
That surely we are approaching
The end of a perfect day.

Where gloom and sadness
Have all been turned away
And sunshine and laughter brighten up the day.

Where friends will greet each other
As in days of long ago
With a hearty handshake
And a friendly Hello!

December 18, 1993

SHARE SOME HAPPINESS

Each day's a new beginning
So we've been told
And at its beginning no one knows
What that day will hold.

For some a day of gladness
For others a day of gloom
As they sit all alone in the silence
Of a lonely little room.

Listening for the phone to ring
Waiting for a friend to call
Watching for the mail that doesn't come
No one seems to care at all.

Family and loved ones
Have gone on before
And they dream of a reunion
Over on that other shore.

It behooves each of us
In any way we can
To share a little happiness each day
With our fellowman.

National Library of Poetry—August 21, 1995

A GOLDEN RULE

I love the early morning
When the world is calm and still
Like to see the rosy sunrise
And hear the first bird trill.

Listen to the soothing ripple
Of the gently flowing stream
See the golden ray
Of the first sunbeam.

A new day is beginning
And we don't know what it will hold
Whether it will be warm, bright and sunny
Or cloudy, damp and cold.

During this day we must do our best
To lighten another's load
One who may be traveling alone
Down a rough and rocky road.

Do unto others
As you'd have them do to you
Is a golden rule we can follow
All our whole life through.

National Library of Poetry—March 19, 1996

PRAYER FOR STRENGTH

Sitting alone in the twilight
At the close of a summer day
And the silence brings recollections
Of a day long passed away.

Far off in the distance
I hear a plaintive Whippoorwill
And continue in my dreaming
Where all is peaceful and still.

And the ripple of the water
Is a soothing lullaby
With its clear reflected beauty
Of a moon high up in the sky.

And as the twilight deepens
Silver stars appear one by one
To twinkle in the heavens
Until the night is done.

As I sit in calm reflection
On some job that day begun
Give me strength for each tomorrow
And the tasks that must be done.

July 1980

Three turtles
Big, middle, and small
Were having a picnic
By the old sea wall.

The sky became cloudy
It looked like rain
Big turtle said
We'll need the umbrella again.

Little turtle said
I know I am slow
But back to the house
For the umbrella I'll go.

Before I go
Just hear my plea
Don't eat the sandwiches
Without me.

They watched a day, a week, a month
A year then two passed by
Big turtle said
We can't wait for the little guy.

Let's eat the sandwiches
He's not coming I know
From behind the rock little turtle's voice came
If you do I won't go.

We can't come in person
Because of the snow
But we are sending "Granny"
To tell you so.

We hope at you house
A while she may tarry
Reminding you of good wishes
From Lawrence and Mary.

The star of hope
In an apple I see
Because it was hid
I thought it couldn't be.

The apple's a house
I had been told
With no doors or windows
But a chimney that's old.

No doors or windows
But a star you can view
If the apple is cut
Right half in two.

The apple
Was put on its side
And with a knife
Cut open wide.

There in the center
For all to see
Was a perfect star
As plain as could be.

Sitting on a vine covered porch
As evening shadows begin to fall
Gently swaying in an old porch swing
Brings a sense of peace to all.

Peace after a busy day
When everything seemed to go wrong
When your eyes were filled with tear drops
And your heart was without a song.

When the world was a gloomy place
And nobody seemed to care
What was happening in your world
If you were happy or in despair.

Slowly the daylight fades
Noises of the day are still
Far off in the distance is heard
The call of the Whippoorwill.

In that calm and peaceful silence
As the world prepares for bed
You find your strength is renewed
For the tasks that lie ahead.

June 20, 1988

I love the early morning
When the world is cool and still
And far off in the distance
I hear the first bird trill.

Stand in reverent silence
Beside a bubbling stream
And catch the bright reflected beauty
Of the sun's first beam.

Hear the crowing of the rooster
And the clucking of the hen
Scratching in the barnyard
For her fluffy brood of ten.

Hear the low grunting of pigs
That have just been fed
As they settle themselves
In a cool mud bed.

Cows that have just been milked
Go plodding down the lane
And the swinging of their heads
Ring bells in sweet refrain.

Sights and sounds of early morning
Make me glad to be alive
And I catch a glimpsed of Heaven
Just a little after five.

July 9, 1988

NIGHT SIGHTS AND SOUNDS

Sitting on the doorstep
In the twilight dim
I listen to the crickets
Sing their midnight hymn

Watch the moon rise o'er the hilltop
Bathe the world in silvery light
See each tiny star that twinkles
Like a diamond in the night

In the calm and stillness of the midnight
Hear the soothing ripple of the stream
As it flows along so gently
And reflects the moonlight's silvery beam

Far off in the distance
Hear the plaintiff Whippoorwill
Then once again there's silence
All the world is calm and still

June 24, 1989

CHRISTMAS 1993

The stars are brightly shining
The snow is soft and white
As I sit all alone
Thinking of you tonight.

The flickering of the firelight
Seems to cast a rosy glow
Over pleasant memories
Of a time so long ago.

In memory I can see you
Just the way you used to be
Warm, strong and gentle
In thoughtful things you did for me.

Although you are gone
You're not forgotten by me
But will live on forever
In my memory.

EARLY MORNING BEAUTY

Did you ever see a meadow
Just when the sun began to shine
See tiny bits of lace hung out
Like clothes upon the line?

Each weed in that big meadow
Became a clothes line it is true
And fairies hung their wash out
For passers by to view.

Each tiny piece of lace
Became priceless too
When studded with priceless diamonds
Etched in by the dew.

The sun shining so bright
The gentle wind that blew
Made a rainbow of color
Just for me and you.

The woven web of a spider
Studded with tiny drops of dew
Created this beautiful sight
That early risers might view.

God and Nature
A wonderful team

May 22, 1988

JUST A PAT ON THE BACK

Each day's a new beginning
Each morning a fresh new start
And it's all up to you
How you play your part.

You may meet someone
Who is lonely and blue
Whose day becomes much brighter
Just by a smile from you.

There may be someone facing a task
That is so hard to do
Who may be encouraged to go on
Just by a pat on the back from you.

Sometimes it doesn't take much
To make life more worthwhile
Just a pat on the back
Or a pleasant smile.

August 10, 1992

LIFE AND MEMORIES

I need your shoulder to cry on
Your arms to hold me tight
Your gentle voice to assure me
Everything will be all right.

I believe we were meant to be together
But a long time before it came true
Then after twelve years
I lost you.

Our life together
Began May 20, 1962
And ended July 22, 1974
The day I lost you.

Now I sit alone
With just a memory
Of the thoughtful things
You did each day for me.

I like to think you're waiting
By an open gate for me
And that again we'll be together
Just the way we used to be.

Sparrowgrass Poetry Forum, October 1997

THOUGHTLESS ACTS

Why do people
Do the things they do
A thoughtless little act
That may hurt me or you.

Refusing to sing in the choir
Because another is singing too
And they don't want to stand
That close to you.

Refusing to sit at a table
Where another is already seated
Is no way that person
Should be treated.

Thoughtless acts of spite
Aimed at one another
Is no way to show love
To our brother.

How would you feel
If you only knew
That act of spite
Was aimed at you.

God put us
All on this earth
And to Him
Each one has worth.

So let's not
Spoil His plan
With little spiteful acts
Toward our fellowman.

June 5, 1996

REMEMBERED THOUGHTFULNESS

When I am sitting alone
Feeling sad and blue
Then it is in memory
My thoughts return to you.

How in twelve years together
We faced days both good and bad
Some that were happy
And those that were sad.

You had the knack
For making things right
On a bright sunny day
Or a dark stormy night.

I remember acts of thoughtfulness
You did each day for me
Someplace to go
Or something to see.

National Library of Poetry—March 13, 1998

Little did I know
On Wednesday April 10th, 1996
I would fall backward down the steps
And end up in this fix.

Lying flat on my back
Before a word was spoken
I knew without a doubt
My hip was broken.

I crawled out front
To be easier to see
Garbage men making their round
Were the ones who found me.

They stayed right with me
While a neighbor called 911
The ambulance soon came
And transported me to U.H.C.

One week in the hospital
Two in Transitional Care
And I returned home
To spend most of the time in a rocking chair.

Doing my exercises
And walking now and then
Were aids to help me
Get back to normal again.

I appreciated all the
Prayers, cards, visits and phone calls
I received each day!

May 4, 1996

QUESTIONS

I often stop and wonder
Do our loved ones know
How we really miss them
In this world below?

Can they really know
The time we've had
If our day was bright and sunny
Or the night was long and sad?

Can they remember
Happy days of yore
Before they sailed away
To that golden shore?

Will we know them
When we meet
And walk together
On that golden street?

These questions
I often ponder
Guess I'll know the answers
When I arrive up yonder.

April 1998
Published by National Library of Poetry and set to music by
Premier Melodies in 1998

AN EXPLANATION

You will probably say I am bragging
And that may be entirely true
But something nice has happened
And I want to share it with you.

I entered a poetry contest
Posted the letter and sat back to wait
The results of the contest would come much later
Before I would know my fate.

Several weeks passed
A letter came
From Premier Melodies
Addressed to my name.

I was filled with wonder
When these words came into view
Our president read your poem
And he liked it too.

The poem was set to music
And as one of five placed in an album too
Now it is all ready
To be played for you.

April 1998

I can see you
Every place I look
Sitting at the kitchen table
Reading the Holy Book.

Working in the garden
Straw hat on your head
Carefully preparing
The first lettuce bed.

Washing windows
At house cleaning time
Too high outside
For me to climb.

Cutting grass
And shoveling snow
Each in its own time
So long ago.

Thinking of happy times
We had working together
In both fair
And stormy weather.

August 1998

MEMORIES

Section II

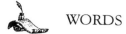 WORDS

We hear words of every description
  As we travel the highway of life
Words spoken in quiet contentment
  Those uttered in pain and strife.

A word to the wise is sufficient
  Is a saying you often have heard
But nothing can cheer a weary soul
  Like a kind and loving word.

There's the cheerful word of greeting
  From friend to friend as they meet
And day after day we hear them
  As we walk the busy street.

There are sad words of parting
  Given to those who are tempted to roam
But kind words from family and friends
  Makes them always remember home.

A word of encouragement sincerely given
  To one who is playing a losing role
May cause him to enter the fight anew
  And thereby attain his highest goal.

God grant that no word of mine
  No matter how thoughtlessly spoken
Will ever bring another pain
  Or cause a heart to be broken.

When you sit down to rest
After the day's work is o'er
Let your thoughts return often
To your friends at the store
Forget the things in your past that are sad
Lift your head, smile, be glad
As you go on your way be happy, sing
And you cares will be light as a gold butterfly's wing.

The star of hope is still shining I know
Just as it did that night long ago
When Wise Men came riding from afar
Guided only by the rays of a star
And found the Babe who silently lay
Sweetly sleeping on the fragrant hay.

May my star of hope continue to shine
And help me fulfill these dreams of mine
May my family and I remain close together
Through both fair and stormy weather
May I earn and keep the respect of my friends
And if one I should hurt, be quick to make amends
Keep me strong to win the fight
To stand for things which I think are right.

As I sit by the window
 And gaze into space
I know there's a guiding hand
 That keeps things in place.

The sun sends its ray
 From east to west
Travels its heavenly course
 Then sinks to rest.

The leaves on flower and tree
 Turn from green to gold
Then silently fall
 To protect roots from the cold.

The animals scurry
 Busily to and fro
Building a food supply
 To last through winter's snow.

Seedtime and harvest
 Springtime and fall
There is a divine time
 Back of it all.

Then if we, like the sun
 Will follow our course
And give the best that's in us

The morning is cool and still and dark
    The world of nature is all abed
Awaiting the signal from the lark
    Heralding the happy day ahead.

A ray of light breaks over the hill
    And quickly moves along
The world all calm and still
    Hears the lark burst into song.

The signal has been given
    The sun begins its daily run
Quickly light spreads across the Heaven
    A new day has begun.

Welcome, Dear Mother
On this, your day.
I know no other
With your gentle way.
One who will cheer us
When the way is rough.
One who will shield us
From each rebuff.
Who, when we need you
Are always near
Ready to aid us
And still our fear.

One day each year
We meet with each other
To sing our praise
For a loving Mother.
This is the day
We have chosen to meet
And lay our offering
At your feet.
This program and banquet
We've planned for you
In deep appreciation
For all you do.

April 5, 1954

A song I cannot sing
   A musical instrument I cannot play
But a little poem I will write
   To tell what I have to say.

What will you do in our talent show?
   Was the question asked at the beginning
I'll give the history of a wonderful club
   In this little tale I am spinning.

An idea for the club was quietly sown
   At a Watch Party for fifty-four
But nothing was done, and nobody knew
   Of the good times that were in store.

Just one month later
   February fourth was the date
Officers were elected at Elridge's Place
   And the group as a club began to rate.

A better community
   Was our aim from the start
So we resolved to work together
   And everyone do his part.

On February 21st at the Lambert's Run Church
   A program was given to awaken the community
That the fun we could have and the good we could do
   Was a golden opportunity.

The Garrett School as a Community Center
     Was obtained by all working together
And now we have a place to meet
     In fair or stormy weather.

At a meeting held once a week
     Where singing and dancing and games are played
We've increased our enjoyment a hundred fold
     With a Juke Box bought with money we made.

If attendance at the meetings is to increase
     We must have a place to sit
A project for the men of the club
     Building new benches, that's it.

If you would like to belong to our group
     And have a lot of fun
Come join with us each time we meet
     You're welcome every one.

June 3, 1954

In a little white church
    That sets on a hill
I worship each Sunday
    While everything's still.

"Safely through another week
    God has brought us on our way"
Is the hymn the choristers sing
    To begin another day.

At the closing of the hymn
    Every head is reverently bowed
As the congregation listens
    To the preacher pray aloud.

Sitting in that holy silence
    Weary souls can find their rest
And each one knows before he leaves
    That he's been fully blest.

In summer when windows
    Are open wide
They let in the sounds
    Of Nature outside.

The sermon is punctuated
    So sweet and clear
By the sound of the Red Bird
    Calling its "wet year".

With a soft rustle of pages
    They find the refrain
And together joyously sing
    God be with you 'till we meet again.

When my task on earth is ended
If I enter Heaven's door
I hope there's a church like this one
Over on that other shore.

Welcome, Dear Father
So loyal and true
These words of tribute
Are just for you
One, who from childhood
Has guided me through
One, who has helped me
In times good and bad
And remained through it all
A wonderful Dad.

Once again November's here
When loved ones from far and near
Gather 'round the festive board
To give thanks unto the Lord
For blessings received throughout the year.

Freedom to worship in a land that's free
A privilege that's given to you and me
Should not be abused
But really be used
To gain a peace that all can see.

Thanks to the Father above we give
For strong houses in which to live
Year after year
Without want or fear
Happy in the peace that freedom can give.

For classmates and families and friends true blue
Our sincere thanks are surely due
To the dear God above
Who taught us to love
And do unto others as you'd have them do to you.

Then let us begin and end each day
Always in the selfsame way
With a prayer of thanks to God above
For His sustaining love
And gentle guidance lest we go astray.

November 1956

I have a friend
    To whom I can go
With a song of joy
    Or a tale of woe.

A steadying glance
    From two eyes of blue
Gives me the courage
    My task to pursue.

When my spirit is low
    With impending doom
His smile is sunshine
    Across the gloom.

When troubles pile up
    Be they big or slight
Two arms around me
    Make everything right.

A true friend understands
    All that we do or say
And matches our mood
    Be it sad or gay.

Dear God, please help me
    In all I say or do
To be worthy of this friendship
    All my whole life through.

August 16, 1956

A new year now is dawning
  Like a page of purest white
And Oh, my friend, be careful
  As you prepare to write.

May you, on your page record
  In type so bold and clear
How you helped a weary traveler
  With a kindly word of cheer.

May many of the deeds
  You have recorded there
Tell how with kindly word
  You helped another, his heavy load to bear.

And should you find a brother
  With head bowed low in sorrow
Will you give him encouragement
  And faith to face a new tomorrow?

In the world of hustle and bustle
  As new friendships you pursue
Don't forget or neglect
  Old friends tried and true.

In the bright new year ahead
  In all you say or do
Try to bring joy and happiness to others
  It will return a hundredfold to you.

December 1956

An apple for the teacher
    Is the gift I bring
I hope that it can measure
    My appreciation for everything.

DEAR GOD, FOR THESE I PRAY

Strength for the task begun
Something attempted
Something done.

Courage in time of trial
Not only to the end
But the extra mile.

Wisdom another to understand
And aid by a smile
Or a helping hand.

Love for my fellowman
A life to live
The best I can.

Strength, courage, wisdom, love
And gentle guidance
From above.

PRAYER FOR MOTHERS

Dear God in Heaven
    Look down on earth we pray.
Send a special blessing
    To Mothers everywhere today.

If one should be discouraged
    By a task that seems too long
Please give her heart a song to sing
    And make her faith grow strong.

Should her pathway be dreary
    Her strength too weak for the last mile
Will you then renew her courage
    By the sunshine of Your smile?

When her heart is filled with sorrow
    And her teardrops fall like dew
Please roll away the clouds
    And let the rainbow through.

Dear God, our earnest prayer
    Is that all mothers everywhere
May know the peace that comes with love
    And knowledge of Your tender care.

TO MY MOTHER

Two eyes shining
    Clear and serene
Two lips smiling
    The sweetest ever seen
Two arms holding me
    Gentle and strong
My Mother understands
    Even though I am wrong.

Those shining eyes
    Tell when she's glad
Those smiling lips
    Cheer when I'm sad
Those gentle arms
    Have guided my way
From my first baby step
    Right through today.

For all that she's done
    I can never repay
But I'll show I remember
    On this her day
With presents and laughter
    Banquets and song
Not only for today
    But all the year long.

In Memory Of The Little Black Pony Who
Died Monday Night—March 26, 1973

Life on earth for you has ended
You'll wear the padlocked chain no more
But roam freely in God's meadow
Over on that other shore.

There no thoughtless owners can neglect you
There our Lord's in full command
And He safely keeps all creatures
In the hollow of his hand.

Daily manna He will provide you
And a drink of water crystal clear
I think I hear you thank Him
As you did me when you were here.

You have found a greener pasture
Where the gentle breezes blow
Where the skies are always bluer
And the crystal waters flow.

If you enjoy a celebration
    Then come along with me
To the Lambert's Run Church
    For our twelfth anniversary.

The first service was held
    On September 13th, 1964
And our hopes were high
    That there would be many more.

The Rev. Mack Bennet, pastor,
    As I remember
Gave us the message
    That day in September.

During this time
    Improvements were made
A piano was bought
    And a red carpet laid.

The inside was paneled
    That is true
And the furnace we bought
    Is brand new.

The funerals in our church
    Have been three
A time of sadness
    For you and me.

The two weddings
    Brought joy and laughter
And a chance to wish happiness
    For ever after.

So at the end of another year
    We hear the old refrain
God be with you
    Until we meet again.

June 1976

We all like surprises
 A fact that is true
That's why we're asking
 Some help from you.

So fix us a package
 Be it large or small
Containing an item
 That will be fun for all.

Fix it right now
 Do it without fail
Send it to the Ziesing P.T.A.
 For their Parcel Post Sale.

October 6, 1975

Don't know how well you like worms
Here's one that will do no harm
Put it in the book you are reading
It will keep your place like a charm.

We greet you this morning
    On Laity Day
We'll worship together
    We'll sing and we'll pray.

We'll open the service
    By singing a hymn
Then be led in prayer
    By our good layman Jim.

Next we'll all stand
    And in unison read
From the back of the hymnal
    The Apostle's Creed.

A special selection
    By the girls from the choir
Fills our hearts with hope
    And a Heavenly desire.

Our speaker today
    Is a layman too
Our own Lonnie Vincent
    A friend tried and true.

When the service is ended
    We'll all say adieu
We hope you enjoy it
    And being here too.

Sitting alone on Christmas Eve
Dreaming of gifts that Santa will leave
Brings memories of days gone by
And makes one realize how time does fly.

As I gaze into the embers rosy glow
I see pictures of the long ago
Home and family, gifts and tree
Just as they used to be.

Shining star atop the tree
Gifts below for you and me
Friends and neighbors who came to call
Friendly greetings to one and all.

As the embers slowly die
One by one the pictures all pass by
Leaving me right back again
Where they all at first began.

December 24, 1982

Did you ever stop to think
The unkind act you do
May hurt someone today
And return twofold to you?

Little acts of spite
That cause another pain
May make the feeling between brothers
Never quite the same again.

So keep a bridle on your thoughts
A check upon your tongue
So you won't regret when old
The acts you did when young.

A poem for you
    I've been asked to write
Here is a sample
    I hope it's all right.

To make a success
    We must all work together
Day after day
    In fair or stormy weather.

In the great scheme of things
    There's a job for each one
You must decide if it's
    Dull, routine or fun.

The mood you are in
    When the day's work you begin
Tells whether you lag back
    Or really dig in.

So let's help others
    Have days sunny and bright
By giving a smile
    To start the day right.

For the happiness you give
    Will come back to you
By doing for others
    What you'd have done for you.

DON'T CRITICIZE

Why do you sit in judgment
And criticize your fellowman
Did you ever stop to think maybe
He does the best he can?

There is an Indian saying
Maybe you should choose
Don't criticize another
Until you have walked in his shoes.

A sunny smile
May often hide a breaking heart
So the world won't know
He is playing a part.

You can't look at another
And tell what is inside
Or the many hurts
He is trying to hide.

Always remember
No matter what you do
The hurts you cause another
May return to you.

July 12, 1997

A TRUE STORY

A little hungry fox
Went hunting food one night
He found a plate of food in the farmer's yard
That filled him with delight.

He didn't know the farmer put it there
It was so good he wanted every crumb
And when the farmer tried to take it
He bit him on the thumb.

The farmer grabbed his gun
No mercy was shown
The little fox died that night
Defending what he thought was his own.

October 2, 1998

REMEMBERING

I remember your thoughtfulness
From the very first start
Of our first day together
Until we had to part.

A white rosebud corsage
My first flowers from you
Was given to me on Saturday
March 10, 1962.

If I had a problem
I didn't understand
You were right there to explain it
And gently hold my hand.

You had the knack
For making things right
On a bright sunny day
Or a dark stormy night.

It's been twenty-four years
Since we had to part
I wish you could know how much
I miss you, I need you, I want you!

October 14, 1998

SATURDAY'S MEMORIES

I remember Saturday, January 27, 1962
The first time you came to me
To offer your sympathy
At the death of my sister Marjorie Marie.

I had seen you often
And knew you by sight
But we had never spoken
Until that night.

You came to buy groceries
Every Saturday at the Chicago Dairy Store
Where I worked in the order department
Every day from 7:00-4:00.

On Saturday March 10, 1962
You asked me to go to a church supper with you
Saturday, April 28, 1962
I received my diamond from you.

Our life together began
May 20, 1962
And lasted until July 22, 1974
The day I lost you.

January 27, 1999
Sparrowgrass Poetry Forum

KEEPING A SECRET

Did you ever try to keep a secret
That meant so much to you
But couldn't be revealed
Until it really did come true?

Well the secret is out
It has come true
And here is a book of poems
For you to review.

To members of the Prospect Press
Each and every one
My sincere thanks is extended
For the fine joy you have done.

With special layouts and illustrations too
The book is a beauty to behold
And worth more to me
Than much fine gold.

December 28, 1998

ANNIVERSARY'S MEMORIES

Thirty-seven years have passed
Since Saturday, March 10th, 1962
When I went to a church supper
For the first time with you.

That was the beginning
Of things we did together
In both fair
And stormy weather.

On Saturday, April 28th, 1962
I received my diamond from you
And we began to make plans
With life together in view.

Our life together began
Sunday, May 20th, 1962
When we both made pledges
To each other we would be true.

Our life together ended
Monday, July 22nd, 1974
When you sailed away
To that golden shore.

March 8, 1999

GOD'S IN CONTROL

When you are all alone and scared
And don't know what to do
Say a prayer to God
He will carry you through.

My prayer before a car trip
Dear God please go with me
Give me the knowledge to know what to do
And when to do it.

When you have a task
That is hard to do
Pray for the strength
To carry it through.

If you are sick
Or in much pain
Call on Him
He'll help you again.

In every situation
Or problem large or small
Our God above
Is in control of it all.

February 22, 1999

MEMORIES

In the hills of West Virginia
    Where the Rhododendron grows
I remember the old home place
    And the love-light that in it glows.

Just a little white farm house
    Nestled among the hills
And going back in memory
    Gives me my biggest thrills.

Hear once more the tinkling bells
    On cows winding down the lane
Coming back to the big red barn
    Because it's milking time again.

Watched the sun rise early in the morning
    When all the world was still
Saw its golden rays
    Creep slowly down the hill.

Listened to the red bird singing
    High up in a tree
Heralding the beginning of another day
    Just for you and me.

Smelled the new mown hay
    Drying in the sun
Feeling an honest pride in knowing
    That works been well done.

Slowly the daylight fades
    The sun sinks in the west
The time has finally come
    For man and beast to rest.

Pray that God who watches o'er us
    Will keep us safe throughout the night.